Original title:
Hidden in the Hazel

Copyright © 2025 Creative Arts Management OÜ
All rights reserved.

Author: Alexander Thornton
ISBN HARDBACK: 978-1-80567-403-0
ISBN PAPERBACK: 978-1-80567-702-4

The Hushed Language of Trees

In the woods where squirrels conspire,
Plants exchange gossip, dressed in attire.
Each bark a chuckle, each leaf a grin,
Whispers of mischief, let the fun begin!

Branches point fingers, trunks sport a smirk,
Roots share secrets, oh, what a quirk!
Dancing in sunlight, branches twist and sway,
Never a dull moment, come join the play!

Reverie of the Twisting Boughs

The boughs hold stories of jammed-up crows,
Who squawk and squabble about where wind blows.
Twisting and turning in a mighty ballet,
Nature's humor, on bright display!

Little birds gossip, perched high up so clear,
Pinecones giggle as they tumble down here.
The sun shines brightly, a cheeky old chap,
Tickling the leaves in a playful slap!

Whispers Beneath the Canopy

Under the leaves where laughter conceals,
The moonlight plays tricks, just like it feels.
Caterpillars chuckle in a leafy parade,
Spiders spin tales in a glimmering shade.

Fungi throw parties where all mushrooms dance,
Frogs croak their raps, giving night a chance.
Fireflies flicker like little stars bright,
Lighting up laughter in the soft night flight!

Secrets Amongst the Leaves

Among the greenery, a stag beetle laughs,
While clever old owls discuss funny gaffs.
Breezes play pranks as they tickle the ferns,
Nature's own jesters, with witty concerns!

Dancing shadows weave tales ever so sly,
While raccoons conspire, no need to be shy.
Bamboo sways gently, a dancer supreme,
Bringing to life all nature's sweet dream!

Shadows in the Glade

In the glade where squirrels play,
They steal your sandwich, run away.
Watch your lunch with wary eyes,
Their little paws are quite the spies.

The rabbits dance, they twist and twirl,
Chasing tails of their fluffy girl.
But when a fox glimpses their show,
They trip on roots and put on quite a row.

The Pulse of the Woodland

Where the owls hoot and wink their eyes,
The woodland beats with silly sighs.
A deer jumps high, a frog replies,
A symphony of nature's spies.

The woodpecker's tap is quite the joke,
As he drills a number on a barky oak.
With every peck, he starts to dance,
Inviting creatures to join the prance.

Secrets Woven in the Green

Under leaves, where secrets hide,
A tiny snail begins to glide.
He's on a mission, slow and sly,
To share a tale with a curious fly.

The mushrooms giggle with delight,
As critters gather for a fright.
Who'd guess the fungi have a laugh,
And share their wisdom on a silly half?

Beneath the Cloak of Wilds

Underneath the berry vine,
A raccoon plots with a slick design.
He tips the jar, sends it rolling,
To fetch a snack that has him strolling.

The hedgehog dons a stick for a hat,
He claims he's "Sir Prickles, fancy that!"
While the badger snores with blissful glee,
Dreaming of treats like honey and brie.

Shadows of the Hazel Grove

Underneath the boughs they roam,
Squirrels juggling acorns as their home.
The shadows wiggle, whisper, and twirl,
With mischief and laughter, they unfurl.

A rabbit hops, in a tiny top hat,
Looking for a spot where he can chat.
The giggles echo, never quite clear,
As the mushrooms join in, sipping on beer!

The dappled light plays tricks on the eyes,
As the hedgehog yodels with great surprise.
A fox provides some curious flair,
With shoes made of leaves, he waltzes with air.

But when the moon peeks, oh what a sight,
A dance party springs up in the night!
With twinkling stars as lights overhead,
They party till dawn with dreams in their head.

Under the Boughs of Mystery

Under boughs where shadows play,
Chickens strut in a grand ballet.
With straw hats perched, they strut with style,
Clucking tunes that make us smile.

A raccoon dons a mask, quite sly,
Selling cookies that make you cry!
With every bite, a giggle grows,
As he winks and twirls his tiny toes.

Beneath the leaves, a secret feast,
A cupcake war, the funniest beast!
Frogs flip-flop, and the turtles race,
While butterflies gather, hiding their face.

Just when you think the fun will cease,
A mouse arrives, bringing fancy cheese!
It's a party where laughter is the key,
For everyone knows, it's all about glee.

Enigmas in the Woodlands

In the woodlands, a riddle unfolds,
With creatures more quirky than tales ever told.
A crab in a hat, dancing on rocks,
Joking with owls and their bright, quirky socks.

A parrot recites the gossip of trees,
Whispering secrets carried by bees.
The owls roll their eyes and flap in retreat,
As the raccoon starts playing the tambourine beat.

Fungi are plotting a musical show,
With toadstools dancing to and fro.
The hedgehogs cheer with glee in their eyes,
While the mushrooms offer their homemade pies.

So gather around, come one, come all,
For in every riddle, there's laughter to call.
With each twist and turn in this forest of fun,
The enigmas reveal that the laughter's just begun.

The Dance of Forgotten Roots

Beneath the roots where whimsy resides,
A serpent in shoes takes graceful strides.
With a wink and a twirl, he shimmies about,
Unraveling tales with a jubilant shout.

A beetle, bedecked as a daring knight,
Dons a grand cape for the dance party tonight.
With dreams in his eyes, he lunges and leaps,
While the grasses giggle and the moss softly peeps.

In rows they all gather, a merry brigade,
Mice bring the cheese, while the owls serenade.
And somewhere beneath, where whispers abound,
The roots hold the stories, forever profound.

So join in the dance with each turn of fate,
In a groove so delightful that none can berate.
For when the woodlands ask you to sway,
You'll find laughter is never too far away.

Mysteries Amidst the Leaves

A squirrel with a tiny hat,
Dances where the branches chat.
Little acorns start to sing,
While mushrooms tease with tiny bling.

A rabbit pulls a carrot prize,
In a realm of leafy lies.
Tickling bugs play tag and run,
Underneath the warming sun.

With whispers sweet from trees above,
They gossip 'bout the hawk and dove.
A dandelion drifts with glee,
While ants perform their jubilee!

But wait! A shadow looms so near,
A fox in shades, we flip to cheer.
And in the giggles through the wood,
A party's brewing, oh so good!

Forgotten Paths Through the Glade

A winding trail of twisted tales,
Where squirrels plot their silly gales.
Beneath the roots, a hedgehog snores,
Dreaming of grand, exploring oars.

A path that's lost to human feet,
Is home to critters running fleet.
The flowers giggle, 'What a day!'
While beetles line up for ballet.

In twilight's glow, the shadows dance,
As mushrooms break into a prance.
A turtle thinks he's fast as light,
But falls asleep—what a funny sight!

The owls share laughs, their eyes so wide,
As fireflies light the night with pride.
What secrets hide beneath the sky?
In glades where laughter seems to fly!

The Unseen Life of the Forest

A wily fox in sneaky style,
Wears a grin that's worth the while.
The trees conspire in rusty tones,
While chattering birds steal the drones.

In the underbrush, a surprise awaits,
A raccoon juggling, such funny traits!
The critters laugh at passerby,
They flip and tumble, oh my, oh my!

A badger found a musty shoe,
Claims it brightens up his view.
With every giggle from the stream,
The forest joins in on the dream.

But wait! A bear, so stuck in thought,
With honey dreams that can't be caught.
They cheer him on with shouts of love,
For laughter is what the trees dream of!

When Leaves Hold Secrets

The leaves, they rustle with delight,
Sharing tales 'neath the starry night.
A chipmunk's joke, a wink, a grin,
  Unraveling secrets held within.

Each twig has whispers, soft and sweet,
  While shadows play a funny beat.
A lonely crow attempts to croon,
  As crickets join, a merry tune!

The ladybugs hold fashion shows,
With glittery coats and fancy clothes.
A bumblebee makes quite the fuss,
Chasing dreams on the vibrant bus.

And as the dawn begins to break,
The forest chuckles, wide awake.
With smiles, they bid the night adieu,
  Where laughter lives in every hue!

A Tangle of Branches and Whispers

In the thicket where squirrels prance,
A raccoon tries a clumsy dance.
Branches gossip, leaves give a wink,
Mischief brewed in nature's drink.

A fox, with ego quite grand,
Struts about like he owns the land.
Trees chuckle, shadows play tricks,
In this wild woodland mix!

Owl's rolling eyes see all the spree,
As rabbits hop so foolishly.
A game of tag 'round twisted roots,
Laughter sprouts in leafy shoots.

So let's toast to woodland cheer,
With acorns scattered, drinks unclear.
For in this grove of silly sights,
Nature's heart beats, full of delights.

The Heartbeat of the Woodlands

Beneath the boughs a heartbeat thumps,
As squirrels leap and tease with jumps.
A porcupine rolls under the sun,
Claiming pride like he's number one.

Mice with tiny shoes scurry about,
In tiny towns with laughs and shouts.
A party planned on a mushroom cap,
With toadstools for chairs, oh what a trap!

The deer prance around with elegance rare,
While frogs croak out their playful air.
The trees sway gently, a rhythm divine,
As nature's joke, it's party time!

So come and join this joyful crew,
Where laughter echoes and skies are blue.
In every nook, a giggle hides,
With woodland fun, where joy abides.

Enigmatic Encounters in the Thicket

In the thicket, secrets giggle,
While bunnies dance and hedgehogs wiggle.
A fox finds hats left by the breeze,
Trying on every style with ease.

A wise old turtle slows his pace,
Scratching his head, lost in a race.
He ponders deep beneath the shade,
While lizards laugh and darts are made.

Among the twigs, a riddle hides,
Can you guess what nature provides?
With whispers shared, the squirrels entice,
Join in the fun and roll the dice!

So gather close in this leafy lair,
With smiles aplenty and joy to share.
In this quirky nook, life's a game,
And every joke has nature's name.

Oasis of Shadows

In shadows where the sunlight brews,
Lies a tale with giggles to peruse.
A chubby bear in a sombrero,
Dances wildly with a peso!

Bats wear sunglasses with flair so bright,
Flapping about in the moonlight night.
Whispers of hedgehogs spread the glee,
As fireflies twinkle, 'Come dance with me!'

A raccoon, a chef in the cool of dusk,
Stirs up adventures with a dash of musk.
Mystery brews in this sun-specked den,
Where laughter flows and lives again.

So step lightly and join the parade,
In this playful glen where joy is made.
Forever a giggle, forever a plot,
In the midst of shadows where laughter is sought.

The Soul of the Sheltered Grove

In the grove where squirrels prance,
A raccoon dreams of a great romance.
He wears a mask, thinks he's a star,
But all he does is raid the jar.

The owls plot in a leafy nook,
Swapping secrets like a storybook.
"Whooo's the boss?" they debate all night,
While the mice giggle, hidden from sight.

Foxes dance with questionable grace,
Tripping over branches in the race.
They claim their moves are quite refined,
But oh, the laughter they leave behind!

Behind the bushes, a badger snores,
Dreaming of cheese and open doors.
His dreams are wild, or so they say,
In the grove where all the critters play.

Reflections in the Whispering Underbrush

In the underbrush where shadows creep,
A squirrel mutters just before sleep.
"Did I steal the wrong acorn again?"
As the wind whispers, he shakes his head then.

The hedgehogs line up for a race,
With tiny traps all over the place.
"Follow the leader, who'll be the sage?"
They tumble and roll, a woodland stage.

A chattering bird mocks little ants,
"You're so small, do you even have plans?"
But the ants parade with determined might,
"Just you wait, we'll give you a fright!"

Under the brush, the laughter grows,
As critters engage in predictable woes.
In this ruckus, a friendship is made,
In whispers and giggles, their plans cascade.

The Chronograph of the Forest

Time ticks slow in the forest deep,
Where frogs keep time and crickets leap.
A turtle asks, "What time's the show?"
But no one knows, they just go with the flow.

The fireflies twinkle, dancing about,
Counting the stars as they flit in and out.
A hedgehog frets, "I'm late for my nap!"
While the bees buzz by, completely a flap.

Rabbits bring calendars, painting the plot,
"Spring is a notion, but where is it shot?"
In this comedy of time and space,
Every second's a bit of a race.

So let's all gather, no need to rush,
In a world where even the wise choose to hush.
For in the laughter, we find our fate,
A timeless joy that's never too late.

Encounters Beneath the Hazel Sky

Beneath a tree with branches wide,
A chipmunk grins, full of pride.
"I've got peanuts, would you like some?"
But a skunk rolls by—he's less than fun.

The owls flirt with the evening light,
Practicing their best flighty flight.
"Whooo's the best?" they hoot and cheer,
While a mouse snickers, unnoticed near.

Bunnies hop with hops so grand,
Saying, "Who needs a dance plan?"
They leap in circles, what a sight,
As a tired tortoise just takes flight!

All these pals with laughter shared,
In the woods, where no one's scared.
With antics galore, each day feels spry,
Their joy awakens 'neath the hazel sky.

Tales from the Hidden Thicket

In the thicket, secrets stir,
Squirrels plot, their plans prefer.
A rabbit wears a tiny hat,
Chasing shadows, imagine that!

The owl hoots, a stand-up act,
While the hedgehog plays a pact.
Frogs croak jokes, they make it snappy,
Even the fox is looking happy!

Breezes whisper tales of old,
Dancing leaves, their stories told.
A wise old tree shakes with delight,
As branches tickle the moonlight.

Laughter bubbles through the green,
In this realm where fun is seen.
Join the party, don't delay,
In the thicket, come and play!

The Heartbeat Beneath the Foliage

Beneath the leaves, a giggle breathes,
A woodpecker's stave, the rhythm weaves.
The bunnies throw a waltz so bright,
Underneath the stars at night.

The chipmunk drums, a beat so fine,
While raccoons toast with berry wine.
A dance-off sparks between the trees,
Who knew roots could move with ease?

With every rustle, laughter blooms,
The shadows twist and hide the grooms.
The flowers sway, they join the tune,
While frogs conduct beneath the moon.

In this grove where smiles abound,
The heartbeat of joy can be found.
So step in time with nature's cheer,
And let the music draw you near!

Enchantment in Every Shade

In every shade, a prankster lies,
A mouse dons glasses, oh my, what a guise!
Winking at the sun up high,
As butterflies go drifting by.

The wind plays tricks on flowing hair,
With whispers filled with light summer air.
A sneaky snail, a daring race,
All in good humor, they embrace.

A dance of shadows, quite a sight,
A squirrel skateboarder, what a fright!
The flowers laugh as petals fall,
Joining the fun, they heed the call.

Within each nook, a giggle grows,
Life's little wonders, who really knows?
In this lively, vibrant brigade,
You'll find enchantment never fades!

The Lure of the Lost Grove

Lost in the grove, a trail of fun,
Where the ants compete to see who won.
Frolicking in the dappled light,
Chasing fireflies into the night.

An acorn in a tiny race,
Wobbly turtles try to keep pace.
With giggles echoing in the air,
Every creature shows they care.

A hedgehog juggles berries round,
Squeaks and squeals, what joy is found!
A secret party thrown so wild,
Even the grumpy old badger smiled.

So if you venture where it's bright,
Join the frolic, share the light.
In the lost grove, fun takes its toll,
For laughter's the music of every soul!

The Language of the Tree Canopy

Underneath the leafy chat,
Squirrels debate on this and that.
Birds gossip in a feathered fight,
While branches sway with sheer delight.

Roots below roll their eyes,
Whispers of gossip in disguise.
Fungi giggle, soft and shy,
While the breeze gives a gentle sigh.

Mosses chuckle on the ground,
With secrets where they can be found.
Each laugh sown in nature's flow,
A party where no one must go slow.

Storm winds dance with merry cheer,
Swaying leaves in a spirited sphere.
Canopies echo with laughter's tease,
In this wild, whimsical nature's breeze.

Tapestries of Nature's Essence

Threads of laughter weave so bright,
In browns and greens, a silly sight.
The flowers wear their polka dots,
While bees engage in buzzing plots.

Butterflies pull a vibrant prank,
Fluttering down to the riverbank.
A playful stone chuckles along,
As frogs jump in, singing their song.

The sunlight sprinkles playful glee,
On this vibrant tapestry.
With each twist and each delight,
Nature's humor feels just right.

Textured patterns twist and twine,
Creating tales of quirky design.
The dance of leaves, a comic show,
In the forest's warm, sunny glow.

The Serenity of the Forgotten Grove

In the grove where none dare roam,
An owl practices its big wise poem.
Raccoons plan their midnight snacks,
While a tortoise shares its clever acts.

Old branches creak like ancient jest,
As shadows play and never rest.
A squirrel's wiggle, a cheeky tease,
As whispers of green drift on the breeze.

The ferns plot a leafy charade,
While crickets sing the serenade.
An acorn laughs, oh what a goof,
As it dreams of an oak as its roof.

The grove giggles, a secret lore,
An untouched stage, forever in store.
In the serenity, mysteries play,
Wondrous tales in a comical way.

Threads of Nature's Secrets

A spider spins a tangled joke,
In the sun, where shadows poke.
Leaves rustle with a gossip spree,
And the brook chuckles, oh so free.

Each twig tells tales from days of yore,
A history rich, with much in store.
Breezes grab secrets, clumsily run,
Tickling the trees, oh what fun!

Grass blades twist like dancers bold,
In rhythm with stories yet untold.
The laughter of nature, a joyous chant,
In the threads where the wild things plant.

Through this tapestry, so surreal,
We find the humor, the sacred feel.
With every step, surprises greet,
Nature's whispers, a comical feat.

A Tapestry of Woodland Tales

In a forest clad with wit,
Squirrels plot in shadows lit.
Rabbits brew their herbal tea,
Spilling secrets, oh so free.

Foxes dance with mossy shoes,
Chasing after wayward blues.
Owls laugh in the quiet night,
Sharing gossip, pure delight.

A hedgehog sips on berry juice,
Claims it gives a wondrous boost.
The trees chuckle, roots entwined,
Holding tales of every kind.

Each twig a quip, each leaf a jest,
In this woodland, life's a fest.
Gnarled branches play their part,
In the comedy of nature's art.

The Enchanted Nook

In the corner of the wood,
Where the peasants never stood,
Bunnies sport with hats so grand,
Toppling twigs with their own band.

A wise old tortoise brews a stew,
Mixing acorns and morning dew.
With a wink, he serves it right,
Hiccups follow, what a sight!

Deer debate the latest trends,
While raccoons plan their weekend blends.
Every nook has laughter stored,
Nature's humor, never bored.

A hedgehog sings a silly tune,
Chasing shadows of the moon.
In this nook, let laughter flow,
Join the dance, let spirits grow!

Revelations of the Gnarled Trees

In the twist of ancient bark,
Secrets hide just like a lark.
Branches whisper, tales unfold,
Cackling jokes from days of old.

An owl with glasses, wise and spry,
Claims that squirrels are rather sly.
Mossy backs of gnarly friends,
Share their punchlines 'til day ends.

In the rustle of the leaves,
Laughter lingers, joy it weaves.
Each fret and fray brings a grin,
Gnarled trees are where fun begins.

Yet amidst the funny sprawl,
Sleepy hedgehogs hear it all.
With soft snores, they dream anew,
Of woodland jesters, quite a crew!

In the Cradle of Nature's Arms

Nestled deep, where laughter flows,
Nature's cradle softly glows.
A chipmunk in a tiny hat,
Juggles acorns, what of that?

Breezes carry hearty sneezes,
From teasing plants, oh, such breezes.
Ladybugs play hide and seek,
Tickle warblers with their beak.

Amidst the ferns, a dance begins,
Where nobody ever wins or sins.
Frogs croak out their silly rhymes,
As leaves applaud with gentle chimes.

In this cradle, fun is found,
Where joy and mischief spin around.
So come and chuckle, feel the charm,
In nature's arms, you'll find no harm.

Echoing in the Leaves

In the forest, squirrels chat,
Debating which tree is best to pat.
A raccoon joins, wearing a hat,
Says, "I saw a cat, imagine that!"

The wind tickles, leaves burst in cheer,
An owl blinks, "Did you hear?"
Chirping birds gossip near and far,
While rabbits dance beneath the star.

They giggle as the branches sway,
One tiny mouse says, "Let's play!"
A game of tag with a twist of fate,
As acorns roll, it's not too late!

The woods echo with laughter bright,
Under the moon's giggly light.
It seems trees have their own brigade,
In a wild, whimsical escapade!

Stories of the Orchard's Embrace

In the orchard, a pear told a joke,
While an apple laughed till it croke.
Grapes rolled by, wearing a grin,
"What's round and funny? A barrel of win!"

Bugs were jiving on leaves so green,
With a bee wiggling, the best you've seen.
"Oh, to be sweet like honey, I dream!"
Said the funny old walnut, quite the team!

Peaches blushed under bright sunny rays,
While cherries whispered of sweet holiday stays.
Lemons chimed in with zesty delight,
"Let's squeeze some laughs tonight!"

As tales unfolded in rows so fine,
The orchard hummed, all felt divine.
With every bounce and silly embrace,
These fruits brought joy to a fruity place!

Images of the Hidden Glade

In a nook, where shadows play,
A hedgehog thinks it's a fine day.
With socks on paws, he struts in style,
And flashes a grin that lasts a while.

A fish out of water, it sings a tune,
"Fishy business under the moon!"
Frogs leap about with joyful flair,
Chasing their dreams and bugs in the air.

A lizard croons of his lost shoe,
"If found, it'll be a brand new view!"
While mushrooms giggle, all dressed in spots,
Legend states they're heroes, but not quite hot!

The glade whispers secrets, a gleeful embrace,
A place where every shadow finds its space.
With laughter echoing through every glen,
The hidden realms leave joy to mend!

Whispers of the Olden Days

Once in a field, the daisies sang,
Old farmer Joe joined with a clang.
"Let's dance a jig, my cronies near,
Bring out the carrots; let's have a beer!"

The corn stood tall, giving a wink,
"Whoever thinks, has had too much to drink!"
Tomatoes rolled with laughter loud,
"We're ripe for fun, let's make it a crowd!"

A pumpkin chuckled, bright as the sun,
"In this patch, life's never done!"
While radishes plotted a prank on a goat,
All in good humor, on laughter they dote!

So in fields of green, the fun doesn't stop,
With whispers of joy, they hop, hop, hop!
In a patch of delight, the old tales reprise,
Each laugh a treasure, beneath open skies!

Beneath the Quiet Canopy

Squirrels plotting secret schemes,
Beneath the leafy beams.
Whispers of acorn treasure hunts,
While owls roll their eyes at stunts.

Rabbits wearing tiny hats,
Dancing with the flapping bats.
A concert led by buzzing bees,
Oh what joy beneath the trees!

Frogs that croak in funny tunes,
Crooning soft beneath the moons.
Mice in shoes would tap their feet,
To the rhythm of the street.

A party hosted by the leaves,
Where nothing's ever as it seems.
Join the fun, don't miss your chance,
As critters jive and break their pants!

The Treasure House of Leaves

In a palace made of brown and gold,
Stories of mischief wait to be told.
Beneath layers of nature's craft,
Lies the loot of a woodland graft.

Nuts disguised as jewels on a crown,
Kings and queens of the forest, dressed in brown.
Rabbits guard the grand entrance tight,
With their noses twitching in delight.

Berries tossed like confetti bright,
Forests filled with pure delight.
Each blade of grass a dancer's prance,
Invite the critters for a chance!

Look! The chipmunks steal the show,
Rolling acorns to and fro.
With tiny hats and sneaky grins,
The mischief starts, let laughter begin!

Misty Reveries of the Copse

Where the mists weave tales so sly,
And laughter bubbles, oh my, oh my!
Pandemonium among the ferns,
As humor flickers, twists, and turns.

Beneath the yew, a fox tells jokes,
To giggling toads and sneaky folks.
With every quip, the shadows sway,
In this secret theater at play.

A hedgehog's quirks, a porcupine's quips,
All join in hilarious trips.
The trees applaud with their rustling leaves,
As the merry troupe dances and weaves.

Echoes of chuckles rise in delight,
As creatures stir in the soft twilight.
Lost in dreams of laughter's embrace,
The copse, a kingdom full of grace!

Lurking in the Rustling Breeze

Whispers dance in the evening air,
With secrets tangled everywhere.
Breezes tease the branches high,
As giggles float from shy to sly.

A raccoon in a masquerade mask,
Hiding from the questions they ask.
"Oink," says a pig, "I'm just a cat,"
While bees debate where humor's at.

Nuts rolling like the best of balls,
Hold the laughter 'til it falls.
A squirrel throws a nut with flair,
And all the forest cackles in care.

Come join the party in the breeze,
Where every moment is sure to tease.
With leaves like confetti, let's all agree,
The world's much funnier, wild, and free!

Whispers of the Forest Floor

Leaves giggle as they sway,
Queries float in the bouquet.
Nuts converse with mushrooms bold,
Secrets wrapped in caps of gold.

Squirrels plot comedic pranks,
Hiding acorns in their banks.
A rabbit jests with a sly grin,
Who knew the woods held such sin!

Fungi dance, a merry crew,
Telling tales of morning dew.
Trees chuckle, their branches shake,
In this world, no hearts will break.

Footsteps drum like a soft tune,
While the sun plays peek-a-boo.
Nature's laughter, loud and clear,
Welcome to this realm, my dear!

Secrets Linger in the Air

A breeze carries a soft taunt,
As whispers roam, they jaunt and flaunt.
A bug flutters with gossip keen,
Sharing laughs with the unseen.

Tall trees wear a witty mask,
While shadows play a game, they bask.
Beneath the blooms, a giggle hides,
A fox who prances with utmost pride.

The daisies join the fun on cue,
Their petals sway, a delicate crew.
A porcupine rolls, all in jest,
Claiming the title of the best dressed.

Clouds drift by with playful pouts,
As nature's secrets twist and sprout.
In this airy realm, joy unites,
Every laugh sends forth delights.

The Realm of the Enigmatic Trees

Bark has tales of lifetimes spent,
In crooks and crannies, trees lament.
Leaves snicker behind the trunk,
While the roots hold a secret funk.

A woodpecker with a loud bop,
Chasing friends without a stop.
Creepers crawl in a sly way,
Whispering jokes from day to day.

Branches twist in a giddy sway,
Inviting squirrels to join the play.
Echoes dance in the thick air,
Nature's laughter is everywhere.

Saplings giggle, full of lore,
With every gust, they ask for more.
In this grove of quirk and cheer,
Each laugh pulls the joy so near.

Moments Lost Among the Stems

A snail slips by with slothful grace,
Winks at petals in a soft embrace.
Grasshoppers jump, bold and spry,
Chasing the sun with a cheeky sigh.

Among the stems, whispers twine,
With every rustle, a new design.
Ladybugs plot a gentle ruse,
While the toad croaks out his blues.

Peeking blooms catch the eye's glance,
Inviting all to join the dance.
Time flies by on butterfly wings,
In this meadow where laughter sings.

Moments shift, and joy expands,
In this patch of verdant lands.
Nature's humor warms the soul,
As we savor each giggling goal.

The Puzzle of the Woodland Floor

In the woods where critters play,
Acorns roll and squirrels sway,
A dance of shadows, sunlit beams,
Nature's jigsaw, stitched with dreams.

A twig becomes a great big sword,
Fighting dragons they can't afford,
A mushroom stands as a tiny throne,
In this kingdom, they're never alone.

Frogs wear crowns of lily pads,
While ants march on like little chads,
A rabbit hops, it's quite a feat,
With every jump, it's a silly beat.

So tread with care on the forest's stage,
Where laughter sings and wonders age,
For in this puzzle of leaf and lore,
Every secret's worth searching for.

Glistening in the Dappled Light

In patches bright, the sunlight spills,
Glimmers dance on silly hills,
A squirrel dons a shiny hat,
While butterflies flirt with a cheeky cat.

The chatter of the wren feels grand,
As beetles march in a parade so planned,
Frogs perform their croaky tunes,
Stealing scenes from the lazy moons.

A bloom beneath the ferns so shy,
Winks at the passersby, oh my!
While ants are busy with tiny dreams,
Plotting their next ice cream schemes.

With laughter caught in every gleam,
This sun-kissed world feels like a dream,
In dappled light, let's dance and sway,
For in this joy, we lose our way.

Cradled by Nature's Secrets

In shadows deep, the whispers start,
Secrets folded in nature's heart,
A cheeky fox plays hide and seek,
While underfoot, the mushrooms peak.

With every rustle, laughter glows,
As bushes giggle, nobody knows,
The shy skunk dons a mask of flair,
While rabbits bounce without a care.

A wise old owl gives quite a wink,
As squirrels plot their next big drink,
The trees are giggling, feeling spry,
Sharing tales beneath the sky.

In nature's arms, where pranks unfold,
The woodland whispers the tales it told,
Come listen close, with heart aglow,
For secrets thrive where wild things grow.

The Allure of the Quiet Thicket

In the thicket where shadows play,
Caterpillars have the best display,
A rabbit whispers a funny joke,
While crickets dance in a trendy cloak.

The brush is bustling with busy bees,
Whispering sweet nothings on the breeze,
A hedgehog rolls, oh what a sight,
In this thicket, all feels right.

With berries ripe, and colors bold,
The secrets of the woods unfold,
While butterflies host a tea party grand,
Inviting everyone across the land.

So hush, and listen to the tune,
Where even the daisies sway to the moon,
In quiet thickets, fun never ends,
Where laughter lives, and nature bends.

Secrets of the Sylvan Realm

In the forest where squirrels play,
Secrets swirl like confetti all day.
A rabbit dons a hat quite grand,
As he leads a dance in the shifting sand.

The owls are giggling, a wise old crew,
Debating the best way to hoot out of cue.
The trees whisper jokes in a rustling way,
While mushrooms shake hands, 'Let's party today!'

Beneath the roots where shadows twine,
A hedgehog juggles acorns, oh how they shine!
The fairies throw sprinkles with a popcorn pop,
As acorns tap dance, they never will stop.

The Quietude of Overhanging Boughs

Under branches that sway like a hammock,
A snail rides a leaf in a road trip panic.
The crickets are cracking up with their tunes,
While mushrooms giggle beneath friendly moons.

A fox in a coat of flamboyant hue,
Plays peekaboo with the owls who flew.
Silvery shadows and the laughter so bright,
Echo through the thicket, a hilarious sight.

A Journey Within the Leaves

Take a trip on a leaf, it's quite a delight,
Say hello to the worms, they're ready to bite!
They dance on a twig as if it were tightrope,
While beetles make jokes, full of slippery hope.

The grasshoppers bounce like they're playing charades,
While ants hold a meeting in secret glades.
"Who ate my sandwich?" a ladybug shouts,
As a caterpillar whispers, "There's no need for doubts!"

Squirrels form bands with their nutty guitars,
Serenading the world beneath twinkling stars.
Jumping from leaf to leaf, such a game,
In a joyous chaos without any shame.

Marvels of the Leafy Sanctum

In a leafy realm where laughter flows,
A chattering raccoon wears bright purple clothes.
He sips on dew with a fancy straw,
Claiming to invent the best drink in the law.

Pinecones spin tales of the days gone by,
While the hedgehogs race under the wide, blue sky.
Fireflies twinkle like they're in a show,
As the trees sway along, to and fro.

A snail with a briefcase walks with such pride,
Proclaiming, "I'm busy!" as he glides to the side.
The laughter spills over the mossy terrain,
In this magical haven, where giggles remain.

Tucked Away in the Flora

In the bushes a squirrel stands,
With acorns tucked in its hands.
It giggles at passing deer,
Whispering jokes that we can't hear.

A rabbit hops with a painted grin,
Wearing a jacket, looking quite thin.
He dances on tips, then trips in glee,
Chasing shadows beneath the tree.

A fox with shades and a beret,
Claims he's an artist, sketching all day.
Rolling out canvases on the ground,
His masterpieces, half-paw, half-bound.

In this greenery, laughter is sown,
Where creatures plot mischief of their own.
The forest's quirks are a brilliant show,
With secrets tucked where nobody goes.

A Symphony of Quiet Secrets

In the leaves, a soft tune plays,
Crickets serenade with fancy displays.
A hedgehog plays the ukulele fine,
Singing to the stars while sipping pine wine.

An owl hoots in a comical way,
Suggesting we all should dance and sway.
Bats twirl like ballerinas at night,
While fireflies flash in pure delight.

A turtle wears shoes, oh what a sight!
Trying to keep up, but it's a slow flight.
He grins at the lightning bugs zooming past,
"I'm just enjoying the world, at last!"

Nature chuckles in its secret delight,
With laughter echoing through the night.
In shadows where silliness will thrive,
The whimsical forest comes alive.

The Unseen and the Unheard

A mouse in a bowtie, planning a feast,
With crumbs and confetti, a chaos unleashed.
His friends gather round with plates in paw,
"Who invited the cat?" they nervously draw.

In a nook, a gnome is painting his nails,
While telling tall tales of giant snails.
He giggles and snickers at secrets untold,
"The best things in life are never too bold!"

Behind bushes, a troupe of ants conspire,
Building a theatre by the old campfire.
Marionette shows of twigs and leaves,
"Watch out for the birds!" is what he breathes.

Laughter dances across the dull gloom,
As creatures conjoin in the magical room.
In shadows where oddities can be stirred,
Are whispers and chuckles, the unseen and heard.

Fables of the Forest Heart

A tale of a frog in a bright cowboy hat,
He dreams of the wild, a fierce acrobat.
But first, he must conquer the lily pad stage,
With leaps and prances, he's filled with rage!

Squirrels hold auditions under the pine,
"Bring your best nut!" they declare, "And you'll shine!"
A nutty comedian makes the crowd roar,
With puns about acorns, they all want more!

Bees hum a tune as they skip through the air,
With tiny top hats, they jive without care.
Dancing from flowers to clover so sweet,
Their buzzing turns into a rhythmic beat.

In the heart of this wood, every creature plays,
With fables spun wild in whimsical ways.
The forest's a theater, alive and free,
Where laughter resides under each ancient tree.

Gleanings from the Woodland Shadows

In the woods where critters play,
I tripped on roots and lost my way.
A squirrel laughed, as I did fall,
It seemed to say, 'You've got some gall!'

The owls hoot jokes from oaken thrones,
While foxes snicker in their tones.
Mushrooms wink from earthy beds,
Conspiring with the sleepy heads.

Bumbling bees, with buzzing zest,
Chase dandelions—they're the best!
If laughter echoes in the trees,
It's just the woodland's way to tease.

Leafy branches wave hello,
As I stroll by, moving slow.
With laughter in this leafy nook,
Life's a joyous storybook.

The Essence of Solitude

In quiet nooks where shadows greet,
I pondered life, then lost my seat.
The ground was soft, a mossy bed,
But now my thoughts are upside down, instead.

A chipmunk chuckled at my plight,
As I tried to regain my height.
The trees stand still, but branches sway,
As they find humor in my fray.

Sipping sunbeams, sipping air,
I learned to dance without a care.
In solitude's embrace, I roam,
Yet stumbled on this laughing gnome.

So here I lie, with nature's giggles,
In tangled roots, I twist and wiggle.
Solitude may whisper sweet,
But laughing woods can't be beat.

Whispers in the Gloaming

As twilight fell, the shadows grew,
In whispers soft, the jokes flew through.
The fireflies flickered, made a scene,
While crickets chirped, they're quite the keen!

A bat swooped low, wearing a hat,
'Twas made of leaves, imagine that!
The stars above shimmered in delight,
As I snickered to the approaching night.

The trees conspired, sharing tales,
Of wayward winds and mischievous gales.
While moonbeams danced on silver streams,
Nature's humor stitched my dreams.

In gloaming's arms, I found my cheer,
With every rustle, there's laughter near.
For in the dusk, with whispers sweet,
The woodland sings a funny beat.

Deep Within the Green Haze

In a world where you might just lose,
I found a dance—of silly shoes.
The plants all swayed to a bouncy beat,
And frogs croaked tunes, oh so sweet!

This verdant maze, it teems with cheer,
A squirrel tried to commandeer.
He tossed a nut, it hit my head,
In leafy realms, nothing's well-bred.

With vines that twist and thorns that tease,
Nature's jesters brought me to my knees.
But laughter bubbled, pure and bright,
In every corner, pure delight.

So deep in green, where madness plays,
I found my fun in sunny rays.
For in this haze of leafy shades,
Laughter blooms like wild parades.

Where Light Meets the Wild

In the woods where odd things creep,
And whispers dance while daylight sleeps.
Squirrels argue, a comical sight,
As rabbits hop, hearts taking flight.

With winks and giggles, the shadows play,
Sending the crows up in dismay.
A deer with socks, quite mismatched just so,
Lags behind, too shy for a show.

A chatty frog croaks tales of bliss,
While butterflies plot their sneaky kiss.
The sunbeams tickle the leaves so green,
In this land where mischief's routine.

With every rustle and gentle hoot,
Wisdom's dressed in a silly suit.
Nature's jesters, oh, such a blast,
In this realm, fun is unsurpassed.

The Fables of Branch and Bough

Under branches that droop and sway,
A wise old owl jests at the day.
He tells of tales that twist and turn,
Of acorns plotting—a prank to learn.

The squirrels scurry, each with a plan,
To steal the crown from a slow-witted man.
A nut parade through mossy glades,
As laughter echoes in leafy shades.

The badger rolls in a sumo match,
While hedgehogs cheer, in this wild patch.
Raccoon plays tricks with a bandit's flair,
As blooms explode with a wink in their care.

With every story, a chuckle brews,
Among the fables, there's humor to choose.
In the tapestry woven of jest and cheer,
Nature giggles loud, for all to hear.

Serpentine Trails of Discovery

On winding paths where sunlight hides,
With twists and turns, the hilarity glides.
A snake that dances, swaying so proud,
    Chasing its tail, it giggles aloud.

The path is a treasure—a map in disguise,
Guiding the brave with sparkling eyes.
A hedgehog on wheels—oh what a sight,
    Racing the breeze with sheer delight.

Dandelion wishes float through the air,
While rabbits play hopscotch without a care.
The trails are alive with nonsense galore,
    Where every step opens a door.

So come, take a stroll, no time to waste,
In this realm of quirks, we've made a haste.
Joy rides the rivers, laughter's the key,
In the twists of the trails, wild and free.

A Symphony of Subtle Wonders

In the orchestra of leaves that sway,
Bugs hum tunes, creating their play.
A caterpillar wears a top hat with flair,
While ants form a line with utmost care.

The grasshoppers leap like they're in a show,
With crickets providing a comedic flow.
A snail steals the spotlight, moving so slow,
While fireflies wink as they join the glow.

Together they dance, a whimsical crew,
Conducting joy, as nature's debut.
Each note, each chirp, a laughter-filled song,
In this concert of life, where all belong.

So let's raise a toast to the curious beats,
In the symphony where every heart meets.
Through giggles and beats, life's fun is unspun,
In the harmony held 'neath the vibrant sun.

Glistening Among the Twigs

In the woods where laughter lies,
Squirrels juggling nuts that rise,
Their acorns fall with comical grace,
Nature's circus, a merry place.

Beneath the leaves, a joke unfolds,
Mice tell tales, humor bold,
With every nibble, giggles bloom,
A pumpernickel mushroom's loom.

Frogs leap in a tap dance spree,
Champions of the ribbit decree,
Chasing flies with comic flair,
A croaky duet fills the air.

The owls hoot in wink and jest,
Filling the night, their own fest,
Nature's whimsy, wild and free,
A laugh-out-loud harmony.

Subtle Hues of the Woodland

In the dappled light where shadows play,
A tortoise creeping takes all day,
With every step, a laugh spills forth,
Patience crowned with comic worth.

A raccoon dons a mask so sly,
Atop a tree, he winks an eye,
His sticky paws in a candy jar,
A suburban heist, a woodland star!

Bouncing bunnies in a fierce duel,
Nibbling lettuce as a rule,
With floppy ears, they hop and spin,
A fuzzy race, who'll win, who'll win?

In hues of green, the silliness grows,
Nature's canvas, a riot shows,
Each twist of branch and sway of leaf,
In laughter, find our bright belief.

Echoes in the Underbrush

The bushes rustle, a secret told,
With giggles muffled, laughter bold,
A hedgehog hides in a prickly ball,
His quills a fortress—not small at all!

Beetles marching in a parade,
Strutting grand in colors displayed,
Beneath the ferns, they shake and dance,
An insect party: take a chance!

A fox pretends to be so sly,
While clumsily tripping, oh my, oh my!
His sneaky plans, a tangled vine,
In nature's jest, all's just fine.

From whispers soft, the chuckles swell,
In the underbrush, all is well,
Echoes ring of joy and fun,
In this wild world, we all are one.

Nestled Beneath the Twigs

Beneath the twigs, a treasure rare,
A bear with slippers, lounging there,
He sips his tea with elegant airs,
In fuzzy socks, he has no cares.

A woodpecker taps, a mad rhythm found,
Baking beats into the ground,
A concert held in a hollow tree,
Nature's DJ, wild and free!

Two turtles giggle as they race,
Slow-motion champs in nature's chase,
At the finish, they share a wink,
To hurry up? Not in their link.

Under the canopy, giggles grow,
In the slumbering woods, a glow,
Each creature frolics in playful ways,
Nestled below the sun's warm rays.

Whispers Beneath the Canopy

Squirrels chat about their cheese,
As raccoons argue with the trees.
A fox claims he's the wood's big shot,
While owls just hoot, by rot and pot.

Beneath branches, laughter flows,
As critters trade their silly shows.
A family of worms holds court,
Arguing who's the best at sport.

With acorns launching, nutty aims,
The mushrooms join in dancing games.
Each leaf a stage, each root a friend,
Where giggles twirl, and never end.

So, peek through leaves, don't stay afar,
Join the woodland, where giggles are.
In this fun realm, no one's too small,
For even ants can stand up tall.

Secrets in the Grove

In a nook where shadows play,
Bunnies gossip through the day.
A hedgehog boasts of all his woes,
While crickets pull off tap-dance shows.

Frogs croak jokes with perfect flair,
While turtles move without a care.
The wind blows laughter from the trees,
As butterflies flirt in the breeze.

With dandelions dressed in cheer,
The woodland friends gather near.
They're swapping tales of silly fights,
And how to reach the highest heights.

So join the secrets, don't be late,
The humor here can't help but sate.
In this grove, with giggling glee,
Everyone's silly as can be.

Shadows of the Woodland

In shadows deep where giggles grow,
The critters scheme with tales to sow.
Rabbits leap with jokes to share,
Underneath a laughing hair.

A badger spins a yarn so wild,
While owl just hoots and winks, beguiled.
The fireflies flash with twinkly fun,
A nighttime show for everyone.

With mossy chairs and twiggy hats,
They gather 'round, these merry chats.
A squirrel juggles nuts with flair,
While raccoons make their antics rare.

So if you wander into this space,
Prepare to wear a laughing face.
For shadows here bring joy and play,
The woodland blooms with jests each day.

Veils of Verdant Mystery

Behind the leaves, where laughter lingers,
Fungi host with funny fingers.
A snail races, slow and grand,
While ants throw parties, quite unplanned.

Fairies giggle in the shade,
Dressed in leaves, their outfits made.
They sprinkle joy like morning dew,
With every joke, the world anew.

The brook runs wild with chuckles free,
As it trips over stones with glee.
Each ripple sings a merry tune,
Beneath a bright, giggling moon.

So peek through the veil, don't shy away,
Where every critter wants to play.
In this lush world, so full of cheer,
You'll find the fun is always near.

Behind the Bark

A squirrel dressed in red, quite a sight,
Claims the tree as its throne, what a fright!
With acorns tossed high, they dance and they twirl,
A nutty affair, in the leaf-swirling whirl.

Rabbits hop by, wearing mismatched socks,
Stealing the show from the shy, grumpy fox.
With giggles and grins, they leap through the grass,
In this silly realm, no moment will pass.

A badger comes out, with a broom in his paw,
He sweeps up the leaves, oh what a grand show!
Critters all gather, they cheer and they clap,
For the best 'garden party' beneath nature's cap.

The trees just chuckle, their leaves in a sway,
As the woodland community dances away.
With laughter and fun, it's a marvelous lark,
In the joyful embrace of the quirkiest park.

Dreams Persist

The owl in a beret gives nightly advice,
While the raccoon debates over cake and rice.
Squirrels in pajamas hold a midnight feast,
With laughter so loud, not even the least.

Each dreamers' delight, a wacky affair,
With chipmunks discussing their latest hair flair.
The moon grins wide, a curious ally,
As critters spin tales 'neath the twinkling sky.

A hedgehog recites Shakespeare's best plot,
While all of the ants work, despite being fraught.
In the heart of the night, imagination flows,
With dreams taking flight, like a wild river grows.

Their giggles and whispers blend with the breeze,
In the twilight of woods, joys are sure to tease.
With dreams that persist and laughter that sings,
In this silly domain, all woodland life brings.

Dreamscapes of the Woodland Realm

In a glade full of wonder, the flowers take flight,
With bees as their pilots, oh, what a sight!
The sunbeams play tricks, through the branches they peek,
Turning whispers to giggles, as leaf critters squeak.

Mice have a party, with cheese on their heads,
While fireflies twinkle like fairy tale threads.
Each leaf like a stage, where the world does perform,
In the woodlands so wild, it's the norm to adore.

The toads wear top hats and sing with delight,
While hedgehogs are jiving, oh what a night!
Each wrinkle and crease in the bark tells a tale,
Of adventures quite funny, across hills and dale.

Dreamscapes unfold, in the soft glowing night,
With laughter resounding, everything feels right.
Among the lush shadows, all creatures convene,
In a world full of whimsy, where nothing is mean.

Nature's Gentle Confidants

The trees share their secrets with swaying delight,
While the dandelions gossip till the morning light.
With whispers so soft, as zephyrs embrace,
They weave funny tales, in this green, sacred space.

A turtle in shades leisurely strolls by,
While the crows crack jokes up high in the sky.
Nature's confidants chat, from leaf to the root,
Spinning tales of wildness in playful pursuit.

The mushrooms sport hats, with colors so grand,
While the sparrows recite a comedic band.
Chasing shadows of laughter, they flit with such zest,
In the realm of the woodland, where humor is blessed.

Each creature a player in this life-so-keen,
With antics so charming, you'd think they were seen.
Nature's gentle confidants weave joy all around,
In the warmth of the green, where the giggles abound.

The Mysteries of the Canopy

The canopy whispers with rustles and creaks,
Where the chattering monkeys plot silly peaks.
They swing to and fro, in a wobbly dance,
Chasing their tails, oh, what a wild prance!

Parrots in feathers, both vibrant and bright,
Play charades with the owls late into the night.
With jokes that are… corny, but laughter, sincere,
In this tangled-up theater, there's nothing to fear.

The sun peeks through branches, a spotlight of gold,
On critters combining their antics, so bold.
The mystery unfolds where the branches entwine,
In a comedy realm that's simply divine.

Every leaf holds a giggle, every bough has a smile,
As critters gather 'round, every inch a new mile.
In the mysteries above, where wonder takes flight,
They create all the joys, in the soft, silver light.

The Enigma of the Hazel Tree

A squirrel danced with nuts in hand,
Juggling acorns, oh, so grand!
He twirled and whirled with a goofy grin,
While birds laughed hard at his silly spin.

The branches shook with all their glee,
As leaves joined in for a wobbly spree.
"Why chase the wind when you can swing?"
Cried the chippy, chirpy little thing.

A rabbit hopped, adorned with a hat,
"I'm off to tea!" he said, so sprat.
With biscuits tucked and music near,
They danced like loons, then disappeared!

In laughter's bloom, shadows roam,
With all things silly, the forest calls home.
Giggles echo where secrets play,
In this wood's heart, every day is May!

Lost in Nature's Embrace

A bear in specs, lost in his book,
Found joy in a napping nook.
A butterfly laughed as she flew by,
"You can't read dreams, give it a try!"

The tree trunks giggled, roots entwined,
As wandering critters shared their mind.
"To find the nut, or have a snack?"
A raccoon paused, then ran right back!

A fox in shades, so cool and sly,
Pretended to be the forest's eye.
"Who knew that bushes can wear such flair?"
With a flick of his tail, he dashed from there.

In nature's clutch, it's quite the show,
Where laughter blooms and good times flow.
With every rustle, mirthful tunes,
Turned mossy ground to dancy dunes!

Beneath the Leafy Veil

A turtle wore a leafy cape,
Said, "I'm ready for a grand escape!"
With snail companions trailing slow,
They formed a band with some cheeky flow!

A hedgehog pranced, can you believe?
Wore flower crowns just to deceive.
"I'm the queen of this garden wild!"
He chortled proud, like a roguish child.

The mushrooms danced, on tiny feet,
As crickets played a jazzy beat.
"Come join our jam!" the lily called,
And in the rhythm, they all sprawled.

The sun peeked through in a playful wink,
While creatures chuckled, none would sink.
With laughter high, they spun in glee,
Under the sigh of the leafy sea!

Echoes of an Enchanted Glade

In the glade where giggles dwell,
A dancing dandelion cast a spell.
With fluffy seeds and dreams to share,
It tickled toes, light as air!

A woeful snail in a race so slow,
Sang, "I'll win with my dazzling glow!"
But everyone stopped to see him glide,
And cheered him on with joy and pride.

The fireflies twinkled, stars on the ground,
As laughter echoed all around.
"Let's have a feast!" cried an eager crow,
"With crumbs of cheese and seeds to throw!"

In this gleeful scene, troubles fade,
With wits and whimsy, fun is made.
The forest breathed a jovial tune,
As echoes danced 'neath the cheeky moon!

www.ingramcontent.com/pod-product-compliance
Lightning Source LLC
Chambersburg PA
CBHW071833160426
43209CB00003B/286